Contents

Any words appearing in the text in bold, **like this**, are explained in the Glossary.

What are atoms?

Everything that exists, from a glass of juice or a computer to a tree, is made up of **matter**. There are many different kinds of matter. Water, wood, and even your own flesh and bones are types of matter. All matter is built from tiny pieces. These pieces are called **atoms**. When you play with plastic bricks, you can use lots of small bricks to build bigger things. Atoms work together in the same way.

Like these model buildings, all matter is made up of building blocks called atoms.

Did you know?
Ancient atoms

People first guessed that matter was made of atoms around 2,500 years ago. A Greek man called Democritus realized that you could cut matter into smaller pieces. But eventually you would be left with pieces that could not be cut any smaller. Democritus called these tiny building blocks of matter 'atomos'. This word means something that cannot be split up.

Seeing atoms

Some things, such as a flake of skin, are too small to see clearly with our eyes. We can use microscopes to see many tiny things. However, atoms are far too small to see with an ordinary microscope. Four million atoms could fit side-by-side on the head of a pin! Scientists use special sensors to find out how big atoms are.

Different kinds of atom

Many different types of matter make up the universe. Scientists know of about 115 different kinds of atoms. Some types of matter are made up of just one kind of atom. These are called **elements**. For example, the element gold is made up just of gold atoms. However, most matter is made up of many different types of atom joined together. For example, plastic bricks are made up of carbon, hydrogen, and other types of atom.

Some elements come mostly from deep inside the Earth. They can be brought to the surface by a volcano.

What is inside atoms?

When something is really small or complicated, people sometimes make a model of it. The model makes it easier to look at and study. Scientists make models of **atoms** to show what they are like inside. Atoms are tiny, but they are made up of even smaller pieces or **particles**.

Particle types

Most atoms are made up of three types of particle. The particles are called **protons**, **neutrons**, and **electrons**. The protons and neutrons are bigger than electrons. They are always clumped close together in the centre of the atom. This clump of particles is called the **nucleus**. The nucleus is very small compared with the size of a whole atom. Most of the atom is empty space that contains one or more electrons.

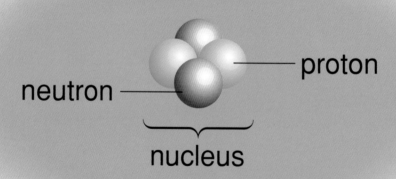

neutron

proton

nucleus

This diagram shows how the particles are arranged in atoms. There are usually the same number of electrons and protons in an atom. The blue haze shows where electrons are likely to be found.

Electron paths

Electrons are the smallest type of particle. They weigh about 2,000 times less than protons or neutrons. Electrons move very quickly around the nucleus. They don't always travel in the same direction or path. You can imagine their paths forming a sort of shell around the nucleus. The electrons are attracted to protons, rather like the way **magnets** are attracted to each other. This keeps the electrons near the nucleus.

Did you know?
Fast electrons

In a hydrogen atom, the electron travels at a speed of 2,200 km (1,367 miles) each second! At that speed it could travel around the Earth in about 20 seconds. It would take a space shuttle well over an hour to complete the same trip.

If a nucleus was as wide as a basketball, the atom it was part of would be very big. You could fit eight blue whales nose-to-tail inside it!

Particles and mass

Mass is the amount of **matter** in an object or substance. An atom gets its mass from the protons and neutrons in the nucleus. The size of these particles is always the same, but their numbers are different in different **elements**. For example, a hydrogen atom has one electron, one proton, and no neutrons, whilst a lead atom has 82 protons, 82 electrons, and 125 neutrons. This means that a lead atom has greater mass than a hydrogen atom.

Particles and properties

Physical properties can be observed or measured without changing a substance into something else. An element's appearance, hardness, and melting temperature are all physical properties. **Chemical properties** describe how an element's atoms behave when combined with other elements. For example, the element sodium is soft and white – these are physical properties. Its chemical properties include the ability to combine with air and water to make new substances.

The particles inside the atoms of these lead weights affect their chemical and physical properties.

CASE STUDY:

Discovering the nucleus

One way to spot something you cannot see is by noticing how it changes the way other objects move. For example, if you threw ping-pong balls towards a blowing hairdryer, you could spot moving air because the balls would change direction. In 1911 a scientist called Ernest Rutherford used this idea to investigate atoms.

Rutherford chose a special element that released a lot of fast-moving particles. He then used equipment to shoot these particles through a thin sheet of gold foil. He put a special screen behind the foil that could detect the particles.

Rutherford thought that most of the particles would bounce off protons scattered throughout the gold atoms in the foil. However, he found that most particles travelled through in a straight line – only a few bounced straight back. Rutherford concluded that:

1 most of each atom was empty space
2 all the protons in the atoms were bunched together in a small clump or nucleus.

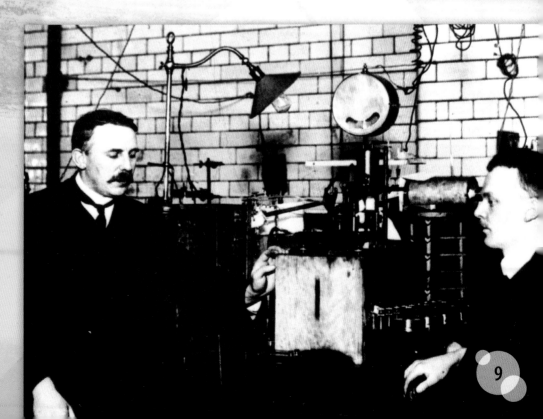

Ernest Rutherford (left) in his laboratory showing the equipment he used to discover the nucleus.

9

What are molecules?

Some **matter** is made up of one type of **atom**. For example, pure gold jewellery is made up of lots of gold atoms. However, most matter is made from groups of two or more atoms joined together. These groups are called **molecules**.

How do molecules form?

The atoms in molecules are held together by **forces** that exist between them, like ropes pulling them towards each other. These connections are called **bonds**.

The bonds in molecules are formed by **electrons**. Some of the outermost electrons in an atom are held very loosely. They can move from one atom to another. Sometimes the atoms share electrons. The sharing or exchange creates a pulling force between different atoms. This pull is a bit like the magnetic attraction between two **magnets**.

These trains are made from a lot of units called carriages. Many sorts of matter are made from repeating units called molecules.

Easy bonding

Some kinds of atoms form molecules more easily than others. The ability to form bonds is a **chemical property**. It all depends on the number of electrons, **protons**, and **neutrons** an atom has. For example, a hydrogen atom has just one proton and one electron. The proton in the nucleus has only a small pull on the electron, and this means that the electron is shared easily with other atoms. However, a gold atom does not bond (share its electrons) easily with other atoms because there are more **particles** in its nucleus holding its electrons tight.

Compounds

Molecules made up of different kinds of atoms are called **compounds**. For example, water is a compound where each molecule contains two hydrogen atoms and one oxygen atom. A compound usually has different properties to the atoms it is made from. Hydrogen and oxygen are **elements** usually found as **gases** in the air around us. They burn easily. However, water is usually found as a **liquid** which does not burn.

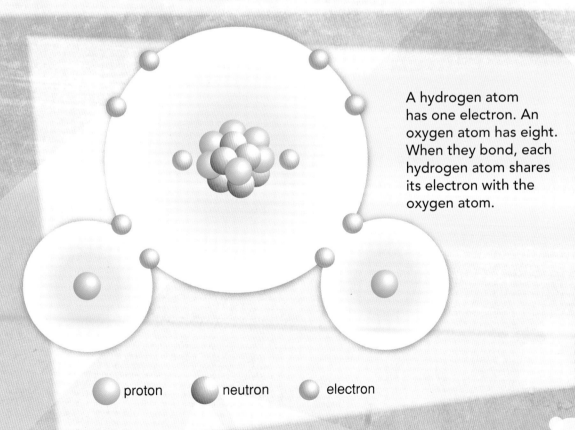

A hydrogen atom has one electron. An oxygen atom has eight. When they bond, each hydrogen atom shares its electron with the oxygen atom.

proton   neutron   electron

Molecule size

Molecules that are only made up of two or three atoms, such as salt, are called simple molecules. Some molecules are complex and may contain thousands of atoms. Examples of complex molecules include protein and rubber. The shape of complex molecules affects their **physical properties**. For example, rubber molecules in elastic bands are long and curly. They straighten out when they are pulled, but spring back into a curly shape when they are let go.

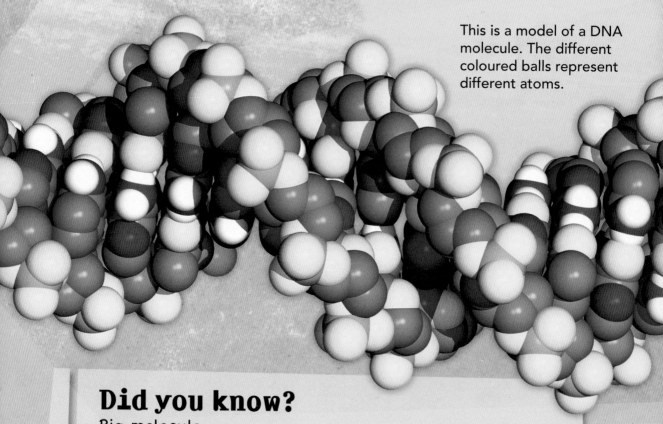

This is a model of a DNA molecule. The different coloured balls represent different atoms.

Did you know?
Big molecule

One of the biggest molecules we know of is DNA. But it is still far too small to be seen by the human eye! DNA is made up of spirals of many different atoms arranged in groups. DNA molecules have a very important job in the human body. For example, they control how our bodies change as we grow up. They also control what we look like.

How do we measure matter?

How would you measure your classmates to compare them? One common way is to put them on scales to find their **masses**. The mass of anything is a measure of how many individual **atoms** it is made from. The space that mass takes up is called its **volume**. For example, a rhino has a bigger mass and volume than a mouse.

Packed together

Comparing **matter** gets trickier when objects take up the same space but weigh different amounts. For example, imagine two blocks with the same volume, one made of concrete and the other of wood. The concrete block weighs more because it has more, heavier atoms packed together in each bit of its volume than the wood. For this reason we say that concrete has a greater **density** than wood. Different **elements** have different densities which affect what they are used for. For example, lead is a very dense **metal** so it is used to make weights.

Pieces of wood and cotton wool with different volumes have the same mass.

Floating

Density describes how much mass there is in each bit of space something takes up. The density of water is 1,000 kg (2,200 pounds) per cubic metre. Objects float in water if they are less dense than water. They sink if they are denser. A lump of metal sinks in water but the same lump flattened and shaped into a boat floats. This is because the boat shape traps air inside, and air is much less dense than water.

Did you know?
Most dense

The densest element is a metal called osmium. It is twice as dense as lead, over 20 times denser than water, and 22,000 times denser than air. This tough metal is often used to make fountain pen nibs that do not wear out.

Air inside vast iron ships makes them less dense. This means they can float.

Demonstration
Sinking canister

This demonstration shows how changing an object's density can make it float or sink.

You will need:
- one clear plastic disposable cup
- large tray
- one empty film canister
- one permanent marker
- fourteen pennies.

Procedure:
1. Half fill the cup with water. Mark the level on the outside of the cup using a permanent marker. Place on tray.
2. Add two pennies to the canister, close the lid and place it into the cup without splashing the water. Mark the level of the water in the cup. Observe the water level on the canister.
3. Keep repeating step 2, adding two more pennies each time until the canister sinks. What happens to the water levels?

The canister starts to sink once the pennies inside make its density greater than that of water. The water level rises up the cup as the canister takes up space in it. Once it sinks, the volume of water the canister pushes out of the way, or **displaces**, is the same as its volume. Displacement is a good way to find out the volume of any object.

What are solids, liquids, and gases?

Any type of **matter** can exist in three different **states**. **Solids** are usually hard or rigid, like rock. **Liquids**, like water, flow and pour. **Gases**, like the air we breathe, are usually invisible and float. The difference between these states is how tightly the **atoms** or **molecules** are held together. A substance's state of matter is one of its **physical properties**.

Solids

In any solid matter, whether it is a motionless mountain or a flying aeroplane, the atoms or molecules that make it up are always jiggling around or **vibrating** on the spot. It's rather like the way we shiver when we are cold. The movement makes **particles** pack tightly together in an ordered arrangement. This means that solids remain the same shape and have a definite **volume**.

These marbles show how tightly packed atoms or molecules might look inside a solid **metal** bar.

Did you know?
Quartz time

Molecules of some quartz crystals always vibrate 100,000 times per second when electricity passes through them. People use this physical property in quartz clocks. When a special device has counted 100,000 vibrations of a crystal, it changes the numbers on the display or moves the hands around by one second. It adds up the seconds to change minutes, hours, days, months, and years.

quartz crystal

Molecules inside a tiny quartz crystal vibrate to change the time shown on a quartz watch.

Type of solids

Solids have different hardnesses. For example, a diamond is hard but a lump of plasticine is soft. Hard solids have stronger **forces** between their particles than soft solids. Substances such as sponge crush easily because they have a lot of air gaps inside. Their molecules make them spring back into shape. Some solids, such as dry sand, can be poured like liquids. However, the molecules inside tiny grains of rock are just as tightly packed as they would be in a boulder.

Liquids

The most obvious difference between solids and liquids is that liquids can be poured. Liquids can flow because the atoms or molecules within them are held together more weakly than in solids. This means they can move from place to place inside the container they are in. This physical property explains why liquids do not have a fixed shape.

Particles in a liquid vibrate more than those in a solid. This is because they have more energy. This energy overcomes the force that holds the molecules together. They are still close together but not in a pattern. The molecules then flow over each other easily. That's why water spreads across a wide area if you spill it.

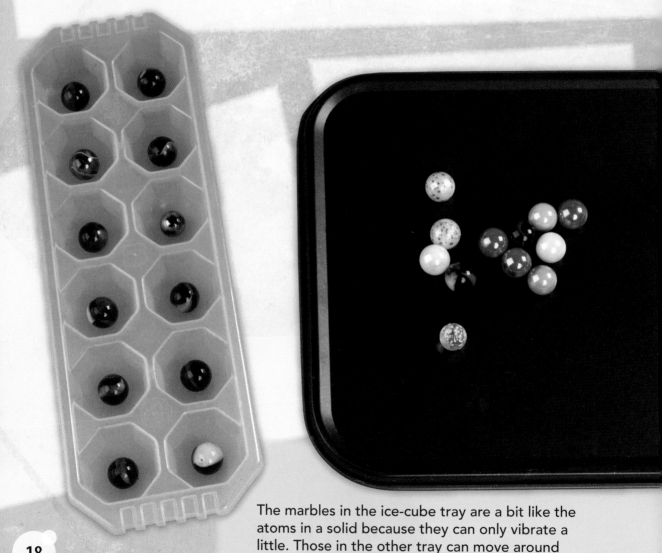

The marbles in the ice-cube tray are a bit like the atoms in a solid because they can only vibrate a little. Those in the other tray can move around much more in their container, like a liquid.

Thin and thick liquids

The thickness of a liquid is called its **viscosity**. It is a measure of how easily it flows. Substances are less viscous when forces holding their particles together are weak, and more viscous when these forces are stronger.

Some liquids, such as honey, become less viscous when they are heated. The reason is that molecules vibrate more when they get hotter. Heat energy makes them move around and crash into each other more.

Honey is so viscous that it can pile up for a short time before flowing slowly to the shape of a container.

Did you know?
Runny roads

Pitch, also known as tar or bitumen, is a black substance. It is often used to make hard road surfaces. Pitch appears solid and can be shattered if it is hit sharply. However, it is actually a very, very viscous liquid. Like other liquids it can drip, but very slowly. As an experiment, scientists set up some pitch in a funnel. Since 1930, only eight drops have dripped out!

Demonstration
Magic liquid

This is a demonstration of the power of forces between molecules in a substance.

You will need:
- one bowl
- some cornflour
- one tablespoon
- stirring spoon

Procedure:
1 Put eight tablespoons of cornflour in a large bowl.
2 Stir in four tablespoons of water slowly using a spoon, a little at a time, so you don't get any lumps. This produces a white liquid mixture.

Slowly stir the mix and it flows like a liquid. Dip your fingers in slowly and when you take them out they get a white coating that drips off. However, when you quickly grab the mixture, you can pick up a handful. You can press it into a ball and roll it between your hands. Punch the surface and it feels hard. The reason is that the cornflour molecules stick together when they move fast against each other.

Gases

Gases have the weakest forces holding particles together. The atoms or molecules move fast. They vibrate, spin, spread out, and press against everything around them. The volume of a gas becomes the same as the container it is in.

Gas atoms or molecules have large spaces between them. You can push them together by putting the gas in a smaller container. The particles hit the sides of the small container more often, and the **pressure** of the gas has increased. When you open the valve of a bike tyre, the high-pressure air rushes out as its molecules try to spread out again.

Did you know?
Floating balloons

Helium is used in party balloons and in airships to keep them in the air. This gas floats because it is less dense than air. Hot air balloons use burners to heat air, which is a mixture of gases, inside the balloon. Warm air is less dense than cold air. It also creates more pressure, because the molecules move faster and are more spaced out.

This hot air balloon will rise and float once the burner has warmed the air inside it.

When does matter change state?

Atoms and **molecules** move around at different speeds in different **states** of **matter**. They move slowly in **solids** and fast in **gases**. It takes energy to move anything. The most common form of energy is heat. Matter changes state when heat is added or taken away from it. For example, a solid can be heated until it forms a **liquid** and then a gas.

Heating and melting

Melting is the change of state from solid to liquid. Heating a solid, such as ice or wax, makes its molecules **vibrate** faster. They start to pull further apart from each other. Substances melt when **particles** move fast enough to overcome the **force** holding their atoms or molecules together.

Mountaineers in cold places get water to drink by heating snow to melt it.

Heating and evaporation

The change of state from liquid to gas is called **evaporation**. Heating a liquid gives the particles even more energy to move around. They bump into each other more often and at greater speeds. Some move so fast that they fly off the liquid surface into the air. Other particles form bubbles of gas. You may have seen bubbles like this in a pan of hot water for cooking eggs or pasta. The bubbles start at the bottom, nearest the heat, and rise to the surface. This is because gas is less **dense** than liquid. Steam or **water vapour** is the gas state of water.

The clouds high above the ocean form when water evaporates from its surface.

Did you know?
Shortcuts

Some substances change directly from solid to gas without a liquid state in between. This type of shortcut is called sublimation. For example, carbon dioxide sublimes from a solid, often called dry ice, into a gas.

Cooling

Cooling a substance removes its heat energy. With less energy, particles move more slowly. They start to hold together more tightly. A gas changes state into a liquid when it is cooled. When your warm breath fogs up a cold mirror, it is because water vapour is turning to tiny water droplets. This change is called **condensation**. Liquid may freeze into a solid when the temperature drops further.

Did you know?
Unusual molecule

Water is an unusual substance for several reasons. It is found naturally as ice, liquid water, and water vapour. No other type of molecule exists in all three states in the range of temperatures found on Earth. Solids are usually denser than liquids because the particles are packed together more tightly. However, ice is less dense than water, which explains why it floats.

Water freezes from the surface downwards when temperatures drop.

Experiment
Shrinking ice

Problem: Ice looks like a smaller amount when it melts. Does the amount of matter actually change?

Hypothesis: When a substance changes state the amount of matter stays the same, even though it might look like a different amount.

You will need:
- a spring balance
- a zip lock bag
- six ice cubes

Procedure:
1 Take a clear zip lock or other plastic bag that can be sealed. Seal six ice cubes inside.
2 Use a spring balance to find the **mass** of the bag and record your result.
3 Put the bag in a warm place until the ice melts. Repeat step 2.
4 Put the bag in a freezer. Wait for the water to freeze. Does it look different to the original cubes? Repeat step 2.

Results: Did the mass of water change when it changed states?

Conclusions: Your hypothesis stated that the mass would stay the same when water changed states. Do the results support your hypothesis?

Melting and boiling points

Different substances have different temperatures at which nearly all their particles change state. For example, water turns to water vapour at 100°C (212°F) or above. This is its **boiling point**. Ice turns to water at 0°C (32°F) or above. This temperature is its **melting point**.

Substances such as **metals** have very high melting points. For example, a metal called tungsten melts at 3,410°C (5,500°F), which is about three times the temperature of melted rock pouring from a volcano. Most gases in air have very low boiling points. It would have to get extremely cold before they would condense into a liquid. For example, oxygen becomes a liquid at -218°C (-360°F).

The boiling point of carbon dioxide gas is colder than the average winter temperature in Antarctica. People handle solid carbon dioxide with gloves so it does not damage their hands.

Energy sources

Substances can change state when energy is added to them. For example, ice cubes cool drinks because they take heat from the drink to the ice cube, which then melts. Water left on our bodies after bathing or swimming can evaporate using just the heat from our skin. This makes us feel cold.

Changing but remaining the same

No matter what state matter is in, it is always made from the same atoms or molecules. It always has the same **chemical properties**. However, its **physical properties** change when its particles gain or lose energy to change state.

Did you know?
In reverse

A substance can change from solid to liquid to gas when it is heated. It can change back to liquid and then a solid again when it is cooled. Any change of state is a reversible change – it can change back if it is heated or cooled.

You can smell hot food because of a change of state! Your nose can only detect smells when food molecules gain energy from heat and drift into the air.

MELTING AND BOILING POINTS

This data table shows the melting points and boiling points of some elements. Remember, these are the temperatures at which atoms or molecules change state from solid to liquid and from liquid to gas. You can see that the substances with the lowest melting and boiling points are all gases. The table also shows some temperature benchmarks to compare these with.

Element	Melting point °C	(°F)	Boiling point °C	(°F)	State at room temperature	
Carbon	3,550	6,422	4,830	8,726	solid	temperature at centre of Earth: 8000°C (14,432°F)
Tungsten	3,400	6,152	5,500	9,932	solid	
Platinum	1,770	3,218	3,800	6,872	solid	
Iron	1,540	2,804	2,890	5,234	solid	
Silicon	1,410	2,570	2,370	4,298	solid	temperature of volcanic lava: 1200°C (2192°F)
Copper	1,085	1,985	2,580	4,676	solid	
Gold	1,065	1,949	2,710	4,910	solid	
Silver	961	1,762	2,200	3,992	solid	
Aluminium	660	1,220	2,450	4,442	solid	temperature of pizza oven: 400°C (752°F)
Lead	328	622	1,750	3,182	solid	
Tin	232	450	2,690	2,690	solid	
Sulfur	119	246	445	246	solid	hottest temperature ever recorded on Earth: 58°C (136°F)
Sodium	98	208	890	1,634	solid	
Water	0	32	100	212	liquid	
Mercury	−39	−38	357	674	liquid	
Chlorine	−100	−150	−34	−29	gas	coldest temperature ever recorded on Earth: −89°C (−128°F)
Nitrogen	−210	−346	−196	−320	gas	
Oxygen	−218	−360	−183	−297	gas	
Hydrogen	−259	−434	−253	−423	gas	
Helium	−270	−454	−269	−452	gas	

THE WATER CYCLE

Water vapour rises into the air. It cools as it rises, and condenses to form water droplets.

Some water droplets fall as rain. If they cool enough, they fall as snow or hail.

The Sun's energy makes water at the surface evaporate. It changes state to water vapour.

Rain and melted snow or ice run off the land into streams and rivers. These carry water into lakes and oceans.

This diagram shows the water cycle.

Glossary

atom one of the tiny particles that make up matter

boiling point temperature at which a liquid changes state to a gas

bond force caused by electrons that pulls atoms or molecules together

chemical property describes how a substance behaves when combined with other substances

compound substance formed from two or more substances that has different chemical properties to either

condensation change of state from gas to liquid

density amount of a substance in a certain volume

displace push something else out

electron tiny part of an atom moving around the nucleus

element substance containing one type of atom

evaporation change of state from liquid to gas

force push or a pull acting upon an object

gas state of matter where atoms or molecules are furthest apart

liquid state of matter where atoms or molecules are weakly held together with a definite volume but variable shape

magnet material with the force of magnetism, causing some materials (such as metals) to move together or apart

mass amount or weight of matter

matter anything with weight that takes up space

melting point temperature at which a solid state changes to a liquid state

metal element, such as iron. Metals have similar properties, such as a high melting point.

molecule two or more atoms joined together

neutron one of the particles that make up the nucleus of an atom

nucleus central part of an atom

particle very small piece of material

physical property characteristic of a substance, such as its state or hardness

pressure force against the surface area of a substance

proton one of the particles that makes up the nucleus of an atom

solid state of matter where atoms or molecules are packed tightly together in a definite shape

state form of matter, either solid, liquid, or gas

vibrate shake around on the spot

viscosity thickness of a liquid

volume amount of space that something takes up

water vapour water molecules in a gas-like state

Further resources

Books

Magnetism (*Straightforward Science* series), Peter Riley
(Franklin Watts, 2003)

Solids, Liquids and Gases (*Science Answers* series), Carol Ballard
(Heinemann, 2004)

Water (*Science Experiments* series), Sally Nankivell-Aston
and Dot Jackson (Franklin Watts, 2003)

Websites

How many times would you need to cut a piece of paper in half before
it became the size of an atom?
http://www.miamisci.org/af/sln/phantom/papercutting.html

Learn all about atoms and particles, and find some fun facts
about their sizes:
http://education.jlab.org/atomtour/index.html

You can see live pictures of the pitch experiment described on page 19,
or watch pitch being shattered with a hammer, at:
http://www.physics.uq.edu.au/pitchdrop/pitchdrop.shtml

Index